HARSH REALM

ALSO BY DANIEL NESTER

Shader: 99 Notes on Car Washes, Making Out in Church,
Grief, and Other Unlearnable Subjects

The Incredible Sestina Anthology (editor)

How to Be Inappropriate

The History of My World Tonight

God Save My Queen II: The Show Must Go On

God Save My Queen: A Tribute

HARSH REALM

MY 1990S

POEMS

DANIEL NESTER

INDOLENT BOOKS

book design: adam b. bohannon
Book editor: Michael Broder

Published by Indolent Books,
an imprint of Indolent Arts Foundation, Inc.

www.indolentbooks.com
Brooklyn, New York
ISBN: 978-1-945023-28-6

Special thanks to Epic Sponsor Megan Chinburg
for helping to fund the production of this book.

CONTENTS

FOREWORD

There is this moment in the sci-fi film *Interstellar* where Matthew McConaughey's character, Cooper, takes a piece of paper, folds it in half, and then sticks a pencil through the conjoined halves. He's making a point to his fellow astronauts about time and space and travel and wormholes. Theoretically speaking, wormholes don't exist on earth but they are as cool as 90s pop, rock, and punk music. And if you are the type of person who wants that outer space experience here on this planet, then you must read Daniel Nester's latest collection of poems, *Harsh Realm*, and feel the pulse of New York City in the 90s.

Why? Because this book is a conduit to that time and space vortex of love. Nester, with these poems, folds that piece of paper in half, sticks that pencil through, and fires up the rocket ship and there we are, immediately, in that wormhole, cavorting with cultural icons the likes of Vince Neil, Gary Coleman, U2, Mazzy Star, Sugar Ray, Live, David Lee Roth, De La Soul, Smashing Pumpkins, Sleater-Kinney, Dr. Octagon, even KISS.

But this is not a book solely about music or bands or movies or the 90s in NYC as experienced from a little sublet on Crosby Street at the edge of SoHo. This is a book about the emotional fever that sustains a human being who is ever-presently enamored with the mysteries of the human experience. This is a book that lets you travel back in time with the speaker, into your own heart, stumbling into that heart and vibe of grunge and AIDS and sex and youth and Abercrombie & Fitch and *Baywatch* and tenderness and 1-900 sex lines and getting fucked up hurtling down the wormhole to hold onto something both nostalgic and unsentimental in hopes that when you pop out the other end, you have learned something new from the old, or, at least tasted the old and thought, "Damn, it's better now than it was then."

Harsh Realm is a book that lets you travel into the past because it's not really the past. It is a gift. It's a gift from Daniel Nester, who is working at his highest poetic powers in these poems, for us, so we can pick up the paper, push the pencil through, discard the slender tool, and then jump into our own little spacecraft to let us get to where we need to get. *Harsh Realm* is a masterpiece of poetic time travel that lets us breathe differently, breathe into a time that has no beginning or middle or end; time that is an orb of music and emotion and language and heartbeat and that comes out of an unquenchable desire to love.

MATTHEW LIPPMAN

NOTE

On November 15, 1992, the *New York Times* ran "Grunge: A Success Story" on the front page of the Sunday Styles section. Along with a foot-tall image of Nirvana's Kurt Cobain, the feature included a sidebar, "Lexicon of Grunge: Breaking the Code," which listed 14 slang terms, or "grunge-speak." The terms were based on a phone interview with Megan Jasper, a 25-year-old sales rep at Caroline Records.

Jasper made up all the terms on the spot. "Wack slacks," for example, are "old ripped jeans." "Cob nobbler" is another word for "loser." No correction ran, and for years people walked around Seattle using grunge-speak terms as if they were real. Ironically, of course

The fake grunge-speak term for "bummer" was "harsh realm."

HARSH REALM

My 1990s

begins at the Berlin Wall,
pickaxe in hand, chipping
at graffitied concrete. For
New Year's Eve I smuggle
five friends across East Germany
in a Volkswagen Golf, bribe
a cop with fifty deutsche marks.
At midnight, a crane hoists
David Hasselhoff into the sky
and he sings "Looking for Freedom,"
his leather jacket covered in
string lights. *Stars & Stripes* runs
a photo of us, swigging
champagne. They mistook students
from Rutgers for Germans
toasting the fall of communism.
It ends on a Brooklyn rooftop,
my hands shake in the cold. I hold
on to my aunt Esther's
diamond ring to propose
to Maisie. She's not surprised—
one night in a cab, I told her
I hid a ring in a bookcase—
but part of me thinks she'll say no.
Why did I pick the moment
when everyone thinks the world
will end, or at least our
computers will blow up?
Instead, fireworks pop over

the East River, and we step
down into the steady light
of the indoors, a neighbor's
subwoofer shakes us
out of a layered decade.

[I can't even say punk was important, even as it happened,]

1991: The Year Punk Broke (1992, Dave Markey, dir.)

I can't say punk was important, even as it happened, I mean, at least where we lived, it was mostly rich kids who went to the shows, who could afford to buy the clothes, who didn't have to work and bought all those stupid buttons at Trash and Vaudeville. Then of course by the time punk got to us, it was *ruined*, it was *over*, and we were *posers*, we weren't there at the beginning and we weren't there at the end. Jersey kids like me mopped floors or washed cars, saw the beautiful girls in sundresses and boots and thought they had awful taste in boys who dressed up like they were janitors or rode motorbikes, but took the same commuter trains we did to CBGBs or piled in their daddy's car to City Gardens or whichever shithole we found ourselves in, and years later all the nights watching jocks lock arms and pile on each other, or the sensitive ones who blamed society and turned into sad sad skinheads. It's hard to point to what broke the spell, if punk ever put us under a spell in the first place, while we hung out at the bar, listening to the music.

Nobody gets credit for that.
Nobody writes an oral history of the posers, even when everyone sells out.

Ruby in Paradise, Philadelphia 1993/1999

for Crystal Durant aka DJ Crystal Clear

I lived like a monk on 16th and Spruce, alone, ascetic, unemployed.
Looking back, I should have done more with my time—written
"The Waste Land," perhaps, or read all of Proust. Instead, I rented movies.
Crystal, the TLA video clerk, held court in Docs and long braids,
played *Songs in the Key of Life* nonstop on the stereo
to counteract the nonstop Nirvana on repeat the boy clerks played.
I always got in Crystal's line to rent my tapes, always in threes:
an artsy film I should watch but put me to sleep (*Amarcord, Solaris*);
the movie I would actually enjoy watching (*Under Siege, Basic Instinct*);
and the porno I'd watch as soon as I got home (*Pulp Friction, Edward
    Penishands*).
Crystal never judged my choices. She took the tags, got my tapes,
laughed at my corny jokes. I rented *Ruby in Paradise*, where Ashley Judd
plays a woman who escapes her boyfriend and moves to a small resort
town in Florida to make a new start. She walks around in a nightie,
listening to the waves. In my apartment, I imagine I am Ruby,
drink beer at McGlinchey's until I fall off a barstool, fax resumes
over dial-up to temp agencies. Six years later, in New York City:
Maisie and I ride the 2 train downtown, and there, grabbing the pole
across from us, is Crystal, all Docs and braids.
And she remembers me! It didn't feel awkward at all, I swear,
to introduce my fiancé to Crystal, Queen of the Video Clerks,
who would hand me copies of *Ruby* and *Five Easy Nieces*.

Nineties Catchphrase Cento Sonnet

Let me clear my throat, Sugar Ray. Back in the day,
I would walk five hundred miles just to grab some biscuits.
No diggity, Joe Camel. Now I'm just a Frasier Furby on Viagra,
Way too single-white-female for one libido to tick tock ya don't stop or
Collaborate and lambada with wolves. No diggity. I've got psychic friend
    networks
In low places. But still. Damn it feels good to be a Rugrat,
To be Lord of the Kato Dance, breaking free from the chains
To hold on for one more quid pro quo Clarisse. East Coast or West Coast,
Brandon or Dylan, Rachel or Monica, Michael Bolton or Unabomber,
Cop Killer or American Gladiator, I'm stuck in the past with how we did it,
Damn it feels good to be a Hemp Rope Leprechaun.
There's no Crying Game endings in baseball.
Take my hand, and Rico Suave off to never never land.
Everything we do we did it for you, fanny packs and all.
We've got a John Tesh bomb on this bus, so word to our mothers.

Catchphrases culled from watching all episodes of the VH1 series *I Love the '90s* (2004) and *I Love the '90s: Part Deux* (2005).

The Art of Prose (With Digressions)

Melvins, *Bullhead* (1991)

Today is the day Melville was describing: rainy, and dark, the end of summer. He would have liked doom metal and free jazz, or said he liked it to friends. All the rebel artists were rich children artists once. They saw close up what these powerful shitcans can do. We are not in the wrong place now, at least. Let's batten down something other than hatches. No one marches to a poem. Sure, there are uncanny feelings, and unsettled bellyaches of energy, but silver is just a shinier gray, and if that doesn't work the first time, love, well, stitch it together and we'll unfurl in the same way all villanelles eventually do. The thing itself is not the same as its name. Whatever. Never mind. When King Buzzo sang *Cross man goes like a toad for peace only,* I was standing right in the front pew. Some day, poetry will end its long, long courtship of birds, paintings, mythology—grant-getters, vacations, naps. Mornings of great contemplation at the foot of famous rebels who live in the woods. Someone may write "What is 'feeling'"? Someone answers: "It's kind of like consciousness, dear, except you give it some goddamn value." There have been more perfect moments than that, but it doesn't matter. Like when King Buzzo's sweat hit me in the face when I was moshing with football players and other damaged dudes. Oddballs can stand around and dance like it's the mummers parade, but it doesn't matter when you're in a mosh pit. Kids still plant flamingos and we put dictators in parades now but it doesn't matter. Today is the day Melville was describing, and I drove five hours just to see a lady with a faux fur hat lip-sync for two hours.

And all that happened in a church, no less.
I will have to have prose thoughts someday, too, I guess.

1992: Wallace Stevens' Lost
Road House Commentary

I do not know which scene I liked better: the man in fingerless gloves, uncred-
ited, who cracks his knuckles with barbaric grace, or Jimmy Reno's face as he
glances toward our New Wave femme fatale's erotic dance around a postbeam.
She dances beyond the grimace of John Doe behind the bar. There is also the
bottle-blonde doctor's chimera entrance in a tablecloth dress. But the dress is
not a dress, nor is this anecdote about Memphis. Both remind us that talent is
the mother of balancing star and support, even if the dancer was not the maker
of the dance. Is there no exactness to the broken windshield? Who can drive an
ATV better while sporting an ascot? Those knifebooted men in Canadian tux-
edos strut into the Double Deuce to slow-tempo jazz. They will always smash
their knees, and they will always drop like stones, especially when there's fire in
the night, running scared from Alabama. Memphis never had anything to do
with it. Bawdiness, either. We stitch our own wounds over an orange and cup
of coffee.

Because somebody pays us to do this.
A stop sign always breaks through the backseat.

I met Liz Phair once,

outside the Khyber Pass. My ticket stub reads October 27, 1993,
but I remember that night as cold, almost snowing out. I was 25,
desperate to escape Philly. I'd given up on quote-unquote
"rock music," and listened only to rap (this was its Golden Age,
after all—think De La Soul, Tribe, Public Enemy). Then comes
Exile in Guyville, with its potty-mouthed songs of love and wreckage,
and photos of Liz Phair and her tiny frame in the gatefold,
looking dangerous. Sure, she was attractive, and the critics loved her,
but Liz Phair was not the usual bratty college rock stuff, like
Pavement or Yo La Tengo (I like them now, years later), or
that night's opening band, Lilys (not *The* Lilys, mind you, lest
snobs pounce and correct you). Liz Phair's songs broke
boys' hearts. She played guitar off-tempo, jittery. She was nervous.
The cool rock dudes smoked in the back while a few of us
stood at the front of Khyber's stage like puppies. After the gig,
I introduced myself outside and—I can't believe I'm telling you this—
asked Liz Phair for a hug. Then she gave me one. I told her
she was my new favorite rock star. She said she wasn't a rock
star, she was going to go to graduate school. I said I was, too
(I hadn't applied yet, but still), and for that second Liz Phair and I
had at least one thing in common. Then, my hands shaking—and
again, I can't believe I'm telling you this—I handed her a copy
of a chapbook of my poems I'd printed at my temp job. It was
an amateur affair (legal paper folded in half widthwise), tall and skinny,
like my poems back then (like my body back then as well). Liz Phair
slipped it inside her back jeans pocket and got in the van.
Twenty-five years later, writing this and playing the *Exile*,

my ticket stub flies out of the gatefold sleeve, along with a single strand
of light brown hair. At first I thought it was Liz Phair's hair,
magically reappearing, but realized it was

      mine, from another time.

The Plan Shifted with a Ferocious Snap

Mazzy Star, "Fade Into You" (1993)

I used to fly off tire swings when I was a kid, off my gourd on cheap beer. One time I broke my toe, and I didn't figure out why till I got home. As I write this, some dude in baggy pants wanders around the coffee shop. He holds his laptop like the ten commandments, the speakers up loud so he can listen to a radio show about state politics. He shouts back at the speaker. No one will tell him to shut the fuck up, much less condemn all the politics that passes us by, all the broken bones we need to become ourselves, all the times democracy steals from us. My cousin's husband, for example, hunted wild pigs on a golf course in South Jersey. We're talking deep South Jersey, away from both highways, near the Pine Barrens where I broke myself and landed too hard. Farmers abandoned the pigs and they went feral, grew stiff hair and horns, and now roam golf courses, terrifying businessmen in plaid pants while they tee off.

I like to think that I was once a hornèd beast, a wild boar who wandered the woods, dodged bullets and poison darts while bankers leapt into their carts, spilling Arnold Palmers, twenty miles from Walt Whitman's tacky tomb. One night, driving out in the pines, I shut off the lights in my car, and took on the highway in the dark, quiet, unmediated by light or sound or direction. I held a cold coffee in my hand, waiting or wanting to hit some tree. I waited some more. Then the glow from my phone lit up the interior. It was my child's face. I flipped the headlights back on. I wanted to live. I wanted to live. I wanted to live.

It seems now I have sat in front of this glow for years and never noticed it. I have talked to young people about their problems, their wish to be outside of themselves or back in someone's arms. I never once thought I'd want to push myself away. *I think it's strange you never knew.*

I now know that no one can wink in the mirror without someone winking back. It is, in the end, the worst tyranny I can predict.

Heavy metal did not die in '91

I know cos I was there, but the critics and TV shows make it seem like one day we sported spandex and lipstick and the next day flannel shirts climbed up our torsos like kudzu. And listen, dude, I know, narrative needs tidy endings. But shit was complicated in '91. Metalheads liked Nirvana fine, but people loved Tesla a lot, too. Plus Ozzy's new album didn't blow, and nobody was putting Bon Jovi out of the Bon Jovi business. You don't go back to 1991 and tell Def Leppard or Van Halen to take a powder. Sure, Dokken flew the coop. Night Ranger, too. But nobody begged for a tune that sounded like Boston dry-humped Hüsker Dü to get played every ten minutes. So what we get now is this whole flash-back-montage, Velvet Revolver-type flattening of history. Some suit puffs a cigar and thinks, "Sure, why not have Slash and that dude from Stone Temple Pilots make an album or two?"

It's easy to think heavy metal died off in the fall of '91 when you never listened to Judas Priest in the first place. It's easy to laugh at men in lipstick when you never took mushrooms and saw KISS back in makeup at Madison Square Garden. Or if all you do is brood to Leonard Cohen all day. Or think pure thoughts about form and minor chords, and how Mickey Rourke in *The Wrestler* was realistic about Kurt Cobain ruining his Mötley Crüe's heyday. Heavy metal was just something you saw on TV. Go back in time to September 21, 1991—"Smells Like Teen Spirit" made the lowest debut on *Billboard*, behind Chili Peppers and Siouxsie. Any time you pit truth against myth, myth takes the cake. And the truth is, some of us never stopped making devil horns and the number of the beast never changed. Metal doesn't die because of one song. It tours South America and waits things out.

So, listen, *you* go back to 1991 and tap on Ronnie James Dio's shoulder. Tell him heavy metal bought the farm. I'll be right here, playing air guitar.

That Twat with Jazz Hands Won't Stop Dancing

LFO, "Summer Girls," *LFO* (1999)

We can only spit out what we swallow first. The genius next to you went to a school you can only imagine. Holy Destruction, you think it was called, but of course it was something else. You should have outgrown this, this idea that you didn't belong, since of course you were bred to belong, you were bred to stay and figure out some place to make something or move something from one place to another, as opposed to feeling some ending or lack of purpose. Time held still. You have to embrace the thing to hop over it! You will die and leave everything unfinished. These also spread: oils, humanity. I owe myself nothing. The choreography of my height threw it on a gun. And I walked away. This is how we mention something: we wave it away. This is how we do it: we carve it all up like Abercrombie and Fitch and Chinese food makes me sick. We know how far from houses we are, how many hogs rest inside the barn. My height just sat there. Fair enough. Mathematics without landmarks is useless. The second knowledge dusts itself off—brands it, digs in and evaluations—a time not of fifty tonnes of whatever but how we got these obstacles: how much, how many, how far, how long. It's good to give explicit appraisals, to show all the strands, necessary and sufficient. Flame up the drinks, a pip, a pop, a sequence, a stretch. This is a pill. These are suppositions. If order has no arms, then order zero arms. There is, you see, no similarity of open profits. We carve up the youth and customer it with numbers—lumens, ounces, decibels. All these timbers and what to do with them.

We carve up the youth we can. That twat over there with jazz hands won't stop dancing, even after the music stops.

This Is Not a List Poem

Public Image Ltd., *That What Is Not* (1992)

this is not not a solo it's a motif, / it's not an outro it's an ending / it's not getting you to think it's drowning in an ocean / it's not a great moment it's a double tracked fiasco / it's not live it's Memorex/ it's not pushed further it's where it needs to be / it's not one of the secrets it's cobbled together / it's not a jump suit it's a crotch cover // it's not one of my asshole friends it's The King of Pop calling you / it's not Becky it's unique it's not unique it's Becky / it's not a German TV soundstage audience circa 1971 it's the primal simplicity of our own desires / it's not smoke on the water it's I've got big balls / it's not Frankenstein it's the doctor's creation / it's not doesn't get you straight away it's a bit of a laugh / it's not fancy it's just transparent / it's not peep-toe sandals it's testosterone *au go go* / it's not freedom from choice it's just a bit of reverb // it's not a doggie's dinner it's make it red and trace your hopes into the ground / it's not paring down it's finding what you're left with / it's not a riff it's finding new ways to mechanically distort / it's not a pregnant pause it's a Rickenbacker / it's not phrase it's a variation / it's not retrograde it's unusual motion /

it's not a list poem / it's a prayer

The death of college rock: September 5, 1995

I'm drunk on a Tuesday at the old Knitting Factory
and stumble into Milano's, where by chance
the MTV Video Music Awards is on.
Drew Barrymore presents
the Video Vanguard Award to R.E.M.
and I am 15 again, pogoing in the mud
in Piscataway, hearing Michael Stipe
sing for the first time. I wore white jeans
and a Corona poncho. I cut off the jeans,
chucked the poncho, and wore a *Murmur* shirt
for months. I thought I'd outgrown band worship,
but watching R.E.M. on the screen feels
as if my childhood had won, as if
arty kids everywhere had won.
The feeling does not last.
Not much later, Hootie & the Blowfish
play their hit "Only Wanna Be with You."
If you were able to establish
which songs were objectively awful,
this song would be the index case
against which all other objectively
awful songs were compared.
Hootie wears a backwards baseball cap.
The Blowfish are all in cargo shorts.
As they play, the audience
bobs their arms like they're at a frat house.
And then comes the real atrocity.
After the guitar solo, the Blowfish
stop strumming and raise plastic cups.
"We'd like to drink this to R.E.M.,"

Hootie says. "If it wasn't for them,
we wouldn't be a band." The crowd cheers.
The cameras do not cut to members of R.E.M.
because if they did, we would have seen
their looks of disgust and horror.
This is the moment college rock died,
in case anyone is wondering. The band
plods on, cargo shorts and baseball cap, and
my night ends like most nights ended back then:
I stumbled outside, hazy, unchanged.

Poem Written at Pete's Candy Store
Ending with Line from "Ray of Light"

Madonna, *Ray of Light* (1996)

There were days when it was *so* my turn to wear the black robe.
When it was "Pick on Me Day." I got that. I got the chill between
what I heard and wanted to hear. I heard the *oh-snaps*
muttered behind each face on the L train to work. These were the days
when this worship of authenticity went way too far. Like the poet
who told me not to write about a "riot" unless it's an actual riot.
These days people just send unsolicited dick pics to each other
and start podcasts. But back then we'd wear Doc Martens
and wallet chains and just bling the fuck out. In another age
we wouldn't rock the word "evanescent." Like, ever. Unless
something was hella evanescent. These days, when the radio comes on,
I want to tell each face at the bar, *yo, trust me, home skillet—
there are better jams than whatever this song is playing.* And I feel
there's a riot inside my head when I remember this, how guilty
and out of breath I felt all the time. And I feel like I should have
sinned more, should have exhaled more. I was all like, *no duh,*
we are in the era between the two Elvises, someone just brought
their pit bull into this narrow-ass bar, and you pick this moment
to call for a Madonna marathon? You go, evanescent figurehead
of evil at the end of this poem! *And I feel like I just got home.*

Looks That Kill

Mötley Crüe, *Dr. Feelgood*, 1990

Vince Neil is well known for transforming lives,
for his continued dedication to rocking out,
but he can't read street signs to save his life,
let alone the Torah or tonight's set list.
So Vince Neil just had Lasik. Mötley Crüe's former
singer gets nervous about keeping his eyes open
without blinking, he'd read the pamphlets, he saw the commercials,
Vince Neil was tired of wearing glasses just to drive
or watch his Outlaws arena football team
play on his flat screen. Vince Neil couldn't get behind
the rhetoric of process, let alone the breakdown
of the bicameral mind. Vince Neil tours casinos
with a new drummer, a born-again showoff
who kicks his cymbals with his sneakers
and makes a cross above his head with drumsticks.
Vince Neil really does transform lives,
he is dedicated to rocking out, but Vince Neil can't
see us crying out for him under the lights.
Vince! We love you! Vince!
Look over here with my cigarette lighter!
Vince! I just lifted up my top!
Vince Neil can't see shit.
So Vince Neil got his corneas reshaped
by two laser-powered, oscillating blades,
just to see our flames and bodies,
just to see our brains' fibers radiate
along a cerebral cortex. Vince can now read

the set lists of the same songs every night

and feel the leather vests and notes from the 1980s

tighten up around him, Vince Neil can now see us

shout *Vince! The bicameral mentality should be non-conscious*

and articulate about mental contents through meta-reflection!

Vince Neil can now see us and hear us, he shouts

at apparitions in the fairgrounds, the parking lots

in Rocklahoma and Wacken, Germany, in South Dakota

and Connecticut. Vince Neil transforms lives,

Vince Neil continues, Vince Neil sees, sings.

October 3, 1995

TLC, *crazysexycool* (1994)

For two weeks before my HIV test came back, I listened to "Waterfalls" and only "Waterfalls." It seemed like the thing to do. For two weeks I ate Ben & Jerry's and sang along to a Discman on the streets of Manhattan. It was my Saturn return, my thirteenth month in a Crosby Street sublet. For two weeks, TLC and me stuck to the rivers and lakes we were used to, steered clear of dopey dirges from Silverchair or Bush, or shitty ditties from Hootie or Sponge or, God forbid, anything from Pearl Jam. Each night on a different barstool I serenaded some precious stranger about the price of poetry. When the morning finally came, I wore tight jeans, shaved, and plank-walked uptown from SoHo one last time, kicked broccoli florets down Broome Street one last time, chased waterfalls with three letters on my mind one last time. I remember thinking this would be the most elegant way to die. I remember thinking all that praying didn't help me at all. The results came on the same day as the verdict for O.J. Along Broadway, I saw the jury on a TV screen inside a shop window, then Judge Ito on another screen, then the sounds from windows and cabs. I saw Johnnie Cochran rub O.J.'s shoulders, the relief and rolled eyes. A man inside an Italian restaurant shouted *bullshit* over and over, and someone inside The Wiz said *this is payback*. Two women in business suits sat on a Cadillac hood. A bear of a man who had drawn my blood met me again at the clinic. He was gentle and wore a yellow sweater. I remember bracing for it, and he showed me the word, "negative," on a slip of paper. We almost hugged. He told me to stay safe. Later, I sulked over a cappuccino inside Big Cup. The world had just stopped and lost a half billion dollars. Water usage across the nation dropped because people didn't want to go to the bathroom and miss the verdict. And I got off scot-free.

With people dying all around me, I thought *maybe this isn't about me.*

Lines composed after being told by a poet I should "go out in nature more often and look at chipmunks"

Spin Doctors, *Pocketful of Kryptonite* (1991)

as if // the last thing I want to do in this short life I have // is to wander outside // and encounter some chipmunk // let alone write a poem in which // mythic weight is bestowed // upon a chipmunk // let's say I'm looking out my window // or I take a walk along an uneven sidewalk // a chipmunk comes up // looks at me // smiles in the way // we say animals smile // the end // awful poem // awful chipmunk poem // chipmunk poems are worse than other awful poems // what I really want to do is never see chipmunks // what I really want is in this short life I have // is to never ever see a chipmunk // at least on purpose // and don't get me started on flowers // there was a nun in third grade // very chipmunk-like // she made us memorize all the flower parts

petals // and anthers and stamens
yeah // so // fuck chipmunks

Künstlerroman, 1996

Before I moved to Brooklyn, I hopped
on the L train and, I shit you not,
interviewed the bohemians
of Bedford Avenue, pen and pad
of paper in hand. I asked
if they liked living in Williamsburg.
Most kept walking, ashamed
to be seen with me. Some were nice.
Even the glasses guy from They Might Be Giants
stopped and talked. I lived in a sublet
on Crosby Street, a fifth-floor walk-up frozen in time,
heated from a brick on a stove, rent-controlled
in a building filled with old men.
This was 1995, and Williamsburg
was no SoHo. We had the L Cafe,
Planet (or Planeat?) Thailand, brunch at Oznot's,
open mics at The Charleston,
Styrofoam cups of beer at Turkey's Nest.
And Joe's Busy Corner, where the patriarch
held court outside and cursed through
his artificial larynx. Everyone
in Williamsburg lived on borrowed money.
We walked to the Citibank in Greenpoint
just to use a bank machine. And our landlord
never cashed our rent checks. Like, never.
Months would go by on North Fifth and Havemeyer.
Nothing. I'd watch my checking balance swell
to four digits and start to think, *this is my money,*
not his. So I'd shop at OMG Jeans
or buy new Doc Martens. Then the landlord

would cash the rent checks. A whole year's worth.
All at once. The whole building would shudder.
I can still see myself a year later,
on a summer morning by the East River
with a Strathmore sketch pad, not very humble,
wallet-chained, younger-looking, jaded,
waiting for last night's mushrooms to wear off
and Tops grocery to open. A skinny boy
bums a smoke. I give him a light. I smile.

A List of Famous People I Saw in New York City

c. 1994-2001

1. Chris Burke, "Corky" from the TV series *Life Goes On*, on the corner of Crosby and Broome on my first day in New York. He was wearing tinted glasses and walked down the street, unaccompanied. First day living in New York, 1994.
2. Keanu Reeves, Lower Broadway near Prince, my sister ran up to him and took his picture on a visit. My mom thought he was someone from *The Young and The Restless*.
3. Peter Bonerz, "Dr. Jerry Robinson" from *The Bob Newhart Show* (1972-1978 incarnation), eating pasta at Fanelli's at the corner of Mercer and Prince.
4. Lewis Black, comedian/commentator from *The Daily Show with Jon Stewart*, Brooklyn, Soft Skull Bookstore, after a reading.
5. Paul McCartney, Beatles bassist and singer-songwriter, *Paris Review* party for U.S. poet laureate Billy Collins, accompanied by then-new wife. I held the door open for them. It was September 10, 2001.
6. George Plimpton, same party. He shooed me out of the room with all of the framed press passes to boxing matches from the 1970s.
7. Ronnie James Dio, heavy metal front man, outside Waldorf Astoria, running toward cab.
8. Fred Newman, host of Nickelodeon's *Livewire* (1984) and cast member of *A Prairie Home Companion*, SoHo Guggenheim. He wore very tight pants.
9. Steven Tyler, Aerosmith lead singer, Lincoln Center fountain, walking with lemonade, with a lot of makeup on.
10. Billy Cruddup and Claire Danes, SoHo, on the street, walking. At Canal Street, we went on the same train, the downtown A.

The Last Days of Childhood

Liz Phair, "Divorce Song" (1994)

One daughter sketches a woman and child in front of a portrait of another woman and another child, except she's not even looking at the portrait, she's looking at someone chasing her child as he jumps on top of an armless couch in the middle of the gallery. Another daughter wants to get to the gift shop, because it's the place where you can get replicas of portraits, like of the woman and child, which she actually did stand in front of but did not draw. What she did draw was the couch-hopping boy who had by that time achieved full self-actualization as both muse and artist since he had his own sketch pad with a portrait of his own mother. I can't lift or carry both daughters at the same time anymore. I'm older and they're bigger. But when I go away, *with or without my best intentions*, when I see any little brat with a sketch pad it reminds me of them. That, or those twinkle toe sneakers that light up when kids stomp on the floor. At night I think of all the ways they might die. After our gallery trips, both girls sleep on the couch, TV on, their mouths open, tongues wet, and I stare at them, watching their chests rise and fall. They're talking about Whistler's mother in this Mr. Bean movie, and I know that if I change channels both daughters will wake up. I made a conscious effort to think about how they were alive and safe and still alive and still safe. On the floor, two sketches of mothers and children and couches lie on top of each other. Mr. Bean was mistaken for a doctor, he's suited up, he wields a scalpel. The youngest wakes up, sees all this, whispers *it's scary*. The artist had roped her sister and nephew into sitting for the portrait. The boy was way too big, and seems to slide down his mother's legs.

They sit inside a windowless interior, no light, just an orchid in a vase on a table and, in the small corner, another painting.

Two 90s Poetry Readings

to be read in "old man" voice

I.

Back in the early 90s I met two poets about taking over their reading series in the East Village. Was it an interview? I'm still not sure. Things looked that way. The poets introduced me to the bar owner. We talked about line-ups. Late in the meeting one poet, the man, said that they "hated poets who revealed too much about their lives." He cringed as he mentioned things like "bodily functions" and "confessional poets who curse a lot." I played dummy and thought about how I think of my life as a series of bodily functions and curses. "You know, like S.," the other poet, the woman, offered. "Well," I said, "S. was my teacher and I adore her work." (I said words like "adore" a lot when I lived in New York.) I said this without thinking. (I said a lot of things without thinking when I lived in New York.) The poets backtracked, apologized and I held my ground. (I was younger then, perhaps more eager to stick up for myself.) They didn't mean to put down my aesthetic, the poets said, stammering, meaning exactly that. Now it's twenty years later. I hadn't looked up their names in years. One went to Iowa for graduate school, which he thought was a big deal. He had a book out a couple years ago. His poems make no sense to me. His family has suffered, experienced losses, and so now I know he was covering everything up.

The other had a podcast about fancy makeup and doesn't write poems anymore. I didn't take over the series.

II.

This was the late 90s. The poet I was about to read with asked me to read first, and I said sure, fine, I don't care. Then he asked me to keep my reading on the short side, since he has a new book, and I did not. "That makes me the headliner," he said. I said sure, fine, whatever. I got a drink at the bar. Then the poet asks me to not be too dirty, since his family was there. He points out to the crowd where his grandmother sits, and we both waved. I said fine, sure. But then I panicked. *But all my poems are dirty*, I thought. Just before our reading, the poet said to me "I like your work a lot—it's very mainstream." I gave him a confused look, and he said, as if to clarify, "Oh, I just meant to say that your poems are funny." As it happened, I was writing a new poem in my notebook, which I decided to debut that evening, a poem about a man with the biggest penis in the world, how his pants have to be tailored for him, how he works at an Off Track Betting place, where he sits on this big stool that creaks. He takes bets on races from all over the world.

There were other lines I sort of remember, like how the man's super-large penis causes him to lose jobs, how he is forced to live alone and forage for his food, how he can't even kneel and pray in church. His grandmother told me she liked the poem, which I entitled "Poem," just to be generic, but I should have called it "Poem for the Poet Who Just Asked Me to Read First, Keep It Short, and Don't Read Anything Dirty Because His Family Was There." This all happened in Chicago. The headliner poet lived six blocks away from the bar.

I'd paid for my own flight, of course, because poets always pay in the end.

Mott Street Pastoral, 1996

So I'm waiting outside for a friend in front of a Little Italy trattoria, sweaty in blue jeans and a t-shirt, and the tuxedoed maitre d' is chewing gum, tinny and loud, mouth wide open, talks up passers-by between smacks, and the macho sunburnt man beside him, fidgety and impatient, wafts cologne from his turquoise Fila workout suit, takes hold of his nose hairs with both hands, pauses for a good grip, then *yanks* and winces with teary-eyed glances at his crop, then wipes it on his thighs; and I suddenly feel a tingly itch beneath my balls, turgid and wet, from what I think are mosquito bites, and scratch there, hard, sniffing my hand as it passes my face.

So there we are: restaurateur, mob guy, and poet, and I want to tell the gum smacker my extended Catholic family once sat there and ate his garlicky pasta, and I want to tell the nose-hair-picker my father was a member of the Teamsters (Local 676), and I feel they are telling me, the ball-scratch-and-sniffer, the brute significance of all of us standing there on a warm Sunday evening, when the world slows down enough to ponder such generic, understood things: we all smell the same scents, chew the same earthy stuff, pluck from the same meaty vellum.

And my friend will pull up to the corner, and the tables will fill up regardless, and the indebted will show up and be persuaded to pay.

To the Protest Song Industry in Crisis

Public Enemy, *Fear of a Black Planet* (1990)

Don't say you're praying unless you're really praying. Don't say you're talking un-less unheard melodies can yap them into construction. And don't play dead now, now that every celibate dipshit, every barbershop loudmouth, every weekend wilted-willy warrior and whiskeybreathed weird cousin commands a tiki torch manifesto in their briefcase. Put the lighters away. We've already run out of the truth. They take away our hands, they storm out front, they fail to stammer.

(And this roughhouse aside—stay away from pooh-poohers who say today's tunes are a worthless cause. No gossip magazine can blot out our complaints. And Jesus, sweet mother of monkey milk, don't giggle when the hot stick pokes your haunch—stare forward, like a bouldered calf. Their quiet-car ears will sense a rhythm, a rhythm of—do you hear it?—sweet mimicry.)

Repeat after me: we need an anthem and we need an anthem now. One that will wreck them every time. And they will take all the parts that make it divine, and, sprung from Glories we see every day, somehow make it even worse, as trollable as any religion without design or myth.

This is not such a bad thing, El Bandito. We've got our in-stresses swinging. So yell out any dish-number—you'll run it right there, baby pop. We're all siblings now. We were siblings before this horrible accident, and we'll be siblings mop-ping it all up. Let God's love ruin it. And God's love always ruins it.

The Failed Saratoga Colonic Fable

Sleater-Kinney, *Dig Me Out* (1997)

Sing, oh muse, of the humiliations of Daniel, son of Michael, grandson of Murlin, who brought upon himself countless ills begotten from that one time he dispatched his Honda at the appointed hour for a colonic in the Spa City, because there was no way a Katherine Harris in Albany would inspire confidence, let alone a keester-tidy in Schenectady, or a shake of Voltaire's angry glove among the smug gentrifiers of Troy.

No, to sing the Redemption Song in Saratoga betokened luxury, sophistication, or so Daniel's reasoning went; a China Syndrome beside the Raceway, a Judge Judy near the Graveyard of Champions, an herbal monkey claw abutting Yaddo and the House of Upsets—sing in me, oh muse, of the Swedish woman who held that hose, many were the hoses she wielded, and the men who looked like him.

My god, what did he think he was doing there, legs in the stirrups, eyes staring up at the stars, he who spoke of impurities and office politics, what did he think when nothing happened, nothing until, oh, smack in the middle of Cohoes, and it was there that Daniel, son of Michael, grandson of Murlin, allowed the child of morning, a rosy-fingered dawn, to appear inside a Dunkin' Donuts off Exit 7, a humiliation that may only be referred to in the third person, and to then discover a Saratoga Springs parking ticket under his wiper.

How had this plan shifted with a ferocious snap. How that ticket slapped against his windshield, all the way home.

Hot Blooded

Freddy's Bar, corner of Sixth Avenue and Dean Street

Our horrible rock band practices in the singer's apartment. We have a gig coming up at a Scrabble parlor. Our graybeard singer can't remember his lyrics, and so he will place an easel in front of himself with a lyric sheet. He will resemble a portrait painter singing in front of a horrible rock band. The singer's apartment is filled with framed photos of his girlfriend's naked ass. After drinking enough wine to palliate the pain of covering "China Grove," I suggest we cover a Foreigner song.

In a roomful of naked asses, I explain the story of "Hot Blooded," a song I loved in junior high. I say it's the story of a young girl. This young girl may or may not be of legal age. The singer asks the young girl a series of questions. The lyrics rhyme "read my mind" with "have in mind." It's genius, in short. If we play this, I explain, women will throw their underwear at us. I know that's a lie, and that all I'm doing is holding off playing the singer's original song, a composition for voice and zither called "Snow Leopard's Lament." I strum minor chords on a futon. What I want here—what I want for *all of us*, I say— is to rock the fuck out, and not to play songs for some Poindexters who have to put down wood tiles to clap.

After the gig, the singer's girlfriend complains in her thick Danish accent that she *cannot hear ze words*. It makes sense that she wants to hear her man sing about her ass. Taking a page from literary theory, I explain that sometimes words aren't important, that the simple sound of her husband's easel-aided utterances would suffice. She rolls her eyes and carries her old man's antediluvian teleprompter out to the cab.

We do not play "Hot Blooded." We do play paeans to a woman who can't make out our words. The Scrabble players clap and gaze up at us. It is a gaze known only to players in horrible rock bands, or those who care to remember true failure—wordless, naked-ass failure.

Barbaric, Classical, Solemn

Ellsworth Kelly: A Retrospective, Guggenheim Museum, 1997

Something happens in the sticker bushes
the day of my first kiss, a baseball game under
black clouds of smoke. This is the day of the fire
at the Garden State Racetrack. It burns down
as Mary Prate clocks me from the bleachers.
She chases me into the clubhouse, she smells
the scallion on my breath from supper.
Mary consoles herself in our passion play. She
plants them on me as racehorses choke off in Cherry Hill.
We kiss through all of this, the day disco died, the day
the beat slows down, the night the Latin Casino
burns down in the rain. Frank Sinatra had crooned
beside that highway, Jackie Wilson clutched his heart onstage,
Richard Pryor complained of a shortage of cocaine.
There's this presence that holds me against its cheek.
It sticks close. It surrounds me, it's the hex that tracks me down.
The day after my tongue tastes Mary's, my pant leg
rumples down into my sleep. I could call it a fire,
but I only dream about it, I wait. I could call it a fire
and trample on it, and I could sing it. I still wait
for a parentless view under the sticker bushes.
I will smell the burning flesh and not seek it.
I will roll in the fire and fail to swell.

Hello, Dolly

Baywatch (1989-2001)

Back in the late 90s, when I lived in Williamsburg, doing my part to gentrify a block filled with Polish gangsters, I found a phone jack in the kitchen. I thought it was an extension of our line, but when I plugged in a phone I heard people speaking Spanish. My first thought: FREE PHONE CALLS! Whenever my roommate went to work, I called 1-900 sex lines, sat on the floor between the oven and the sink, and talked dirty to this lady who sounded exactly like Carol Channing. She told me that she had a really great body. "Have you ever heard of Pamela Anderson?" she asked me. I said of course I had, but I couldn't shake from my mind how she sounded so much like Carol Channing. The last time we talked, someone else picked up the phone, like my sister did back in high school, except this lady screamed something in Spanish.

I worked so hard to concentrate, doing what I meant to do, and to think *Baywatch* thoughts and not *Hello, Dolly* thoughts, to keep my lizard brain together in my underwear, next to the oven, my roommate taking his sweet time to come upstairs.

The Drummer in Our Band
Tells Us He's a Virgin

We're arguing over arrangements again, and Albert speaks with heavy reverb in a microphone meant for floor toms. "I'm a virgin," he says, just out of the blue. Everyone stops to look at each other—the singer looks at me, me at the bass player, the bass player looks at the lead guitarist who looks at me, and I look at the drummer. For three years every Tuesday, this grown man with curly hair and Hawaiian shirts has held the bottom of our hard rock combo, and now, as we pick apart each other's inexorable, 16-bar solos, he comes out with such a revelation that everyone turns their volumes down and sits.

One night, I sat through a production of *Kabuki Othello*. I arrived drunk and rowdy, and burped out loud when I heard this demonstrative and overblown Iago milk his lines, a minute alone just to say the word "honest." My head aches just to recall our covers of the hair metal Kurt Cobain supposedly killed. I say *it's OK, Albert. Honesty is the bravest form of music*. The singer agrees. The bassist consummates the chord progression, shuffles his pristine white sneakers, and our virgin drummer wipes his thick glasses clean and takes it from the top with a knock of his sticks.

We play the next triptych from the fakebook and my arm windmills. We're pure again. Metal will return again. We wait for silence, wait for Desdemona to die.

Lower Broadway Wednesdays, 1997–1999

There were Wednesday afternoons—it always
seemed to be Wednesdays—when I would
walk into a public bathroom—an NYU basement,
on a break from work at the film department,
then Barnes & Noble or the Writer's Room
on Astor Place, where I would go not to write,
but to stare at a cubicle wall and experience silence—
and cry, uncontrollably, sound muffled in my hands,
often to the point where my eyes would be bloodshot.
I would walk out, complaining about my contacts
if anyone asked or seemed concerned.
Other Wednesdays I walked to the Bath & Body Works
on Lower Broadway to use the free samplers of hair gel,
and there was always a young guy working there
who would strike up a conversation with me,
never about the hair gels or trying to sell me anything,
but just ask friendly questions. It's only now
writing this that I realize he might have had a crush
on me. One Wednesday while I gelled up my hair
and looked in the mirror, he tried out a back massager
on my shoulders. It felt good. I walked back to work,
feeling—and there's no other word to use here—fabulous.

Nostalgia Ain't What It Used to Be

The Smashing Pumpkins, "1979" (1996)

Because this word contains a world we should use it and give meaning to it. Because nostalgia doesn't mean homecoming. Because it's not just our flat melancholy. It's just compounded memories. We are not remembering the remembering. No rose-tints. No 1979. No transitions between childhoods. I can't communicate from the edge. I can't communicate wearing a turtleneck. So tell me more. Tell me to flip off out of this town. Let's get out of here and forget it for a couple years. I'll call back. You won't be glad to hear from me. That's fine. I'll call it coming close to everything I wanted, which is saying something. Some years are just better-sounding than others. That's a fact. Go ahead and be a hot child in the city. Go ahead and fuse whichever conspiracy you want to with each other. Up and down has patterns, and it gets old, Sister Sledge. I'm through with crying just for me, Action Jackson. It's more about worry over whether you might get hurt. And it's those salad days you want the most. The salads that went with the song. Almost reformed. Almost a house party. I can't look back to what I once was. I ache. I long. I don't look like a girl anymore if I ever did. Today is the day I didn't cry. You think there's a difference between the devil and free spirits. I'm not so sure.

Then I found heavy metal and stupid pants didn't matter anymore. End of story.

I Tell These Stories to Explain
Why People Stop Liking Me

Cocteau Twins, *Heaven or Las Vegas* (1990); Slint, *Spiderland* (1991)

I.

I always find people I need to avoid. Like the poets who interview each other on a couch. They pass a microphone between them like a torch and plant big wet ones on each other after the questions are over. Questions no one else has ever bothered to answer. I always find people I need to avoid and now I get it—all those underground poets use publicists! But I have to make a confession: I did not sleep. Sick of jackhammers, the ballerina slippers, sick of the mother of all days, sick of the hallelujah chorus pedals, sick of the Chuck Berry hot tub pee-pee tape, sick of picket-fences, whatever a picket is, if you feel yourself responding cynically, Camerado, you're with me then—why reel and falter in the face of realness, why be so binary?

I'm the only one left. The storm took them all.

II.

Can you still get Quaaludes? Like, outside Woody Allen movies? Cos I'd like one, a Quaalude, is what I am saying. Sure, I was publicly shamed and reviled, but I'm used to that. I'd been lying low for what? Almost ten years now? How old is my youngest daughter? That long, dammit. So when the brotherhood of the snake rolls up and sings the national anthem, take a goddamn knee. I want some Quaaludes and I want to listen to experimental jazz and poetry records, and that is what I plan to do in my dotage every weekend.

It will be then that I will have completed my life's work, an endurance performance piece we will call "Mediocre Man's Contorted Face."

Eavesfall

It's raining this morning, first as a mist, then mini-waterfalls off the eaves. "Eavesfalls" isn't a word, but it sounds neat. The online dictionaries tell me "eavesdrop" is, however, as is "antieavesdropping." In the other room, Miriam and Bea argue over the use of the single hairbrush we can find. "Do you want waterfalls?" Maisie asks them. That's their word for French braids. They like the way they look but don't like how the tangles hurt brushed through. They scream. End scene. They both walk over to me and start pushing my head from one side, over and over as I spring my head back. I look like I'm dancing to New Wave when I wore handkerchiefs around my neck and I couldn't bear to get my hair wet.

Week One Introductions, 1997

It's the first day of the semester and I've just
slogged through the syllabus. A student walks up
to my teaching station. "I can't look at your face,"
she says. "I'm sorry?" I say. "Your face. When you talk,
it changes too much. It's disturbing. I can't really look at it."
I've been conditioned for so long to please students
that I offer an accommodation. "I understand," I say.
"Will looking at my face be a problem moving forward this semester?"
"Oh, no, you're good," she says. "I'll figure out something."
It doesn't occur to me that what's been said to me is
so audaciously unkind until she leaves. Another student
hands me their sports schedule. Outside, the sky is so blue
I put my sunglasses on and promise myself
to tell no one about this. I keep my face still.

Future Days

Live, *Throwing Copper* (1994)

That one time no one showed up for a poetry reading
I hosted, that one event replays over again up here in Albany,
where no one shows up to any poetry readings anyway
and where the only station my AM radio gets
loud and clear is "Catholic words of peace and glory."
I camp out at the second-string coffee place with high windows
like the Brooklyn bookstore where no one showed up
to the poetry reading. The poets came, sure. They always do.
But no one else did. The poets blamed it on Charles Bernstein's wife,
who had an art opening. Which would've made sense,
but it was in another borough and on another day.
The poets were Canadian, and complained about their
small travel grants. I bought them drinks. Today,
in the second-string coffee place filled with high windows,
undergrads talk about god and test scores, and I spot
a grad student I know, his face in Williams' prose.
He's wrestled with him for years now, says it's like *living
inside a molasses jar*. We talk about the baseball
poem, how the *crowd moved uniformly*, how it reminds me
of the proofreader who flagged phantom pronouns
in my manuscript, the one I'd sweated over for years.
The Williams poem hinges on what "it" refers to—
Is "it" the crowd at the ball game eating hot dogs?
Or is "it" America, the failed experiment?
In this second-string coffee place, undergrads blast rap-metal
and they think it will force me out of my primo booth spot—
Fuck that noise. I got a table, a power outlet, and headphones

to blast Can then Gong then Can then Gong then Can then Gong.
On my screen, phantom pronouns pop in and out. I play
the *Throwing Copper* album, where the guy from Talking Heads
lets slip a second of silence in the middle of Live's best song.
A big mastering fuck-up? Did Greg Calbi not show up that day?
Did he record it in Cannon Falls, Minnesota or who the fuck
knows where? I bet the drummer in Can knows. What could I say
to my shrink today that could clear my head any better?
What problems could I replay to her instead of the one
unifying problem, which is that I hate myself, that I can't say out loud
that I am mediocre, that I can't say I have wasted too many afternoons
like this in search of a poem. Today, instead, I mull over the two-way tie
for the worst lines of poetry I've ever heard aloud.
Number 1: "That was the winter I wouldn't wear wool."
Number 2: "Humberto is delivering breakfast sandwiches."
One's by a former teacher of mine.
The other is by someone from Philadelphia.
Who was the drummer for Can, anyway?
Didn't he just die? Did he practice his breathing?
Alone with my headphones and coffee straws,
passwords written in chalk on bricks gather light from a window,
and I remember the day in the hospital just down the street
from here in Albany, in the second-string coffee shop
with high windows, when my daughter's legs turned blue
last summer, and I couldn't drive straight or walk straight,
and I ran into the room where she was in bed and she was
OK but scared to have her face with tubes in it. My chest
froze there in the hallway, and I touched her small ears
and sang her name a little bit—it was all I could do to stand there,
to appear fatherly, to breathe in and out, helpless and still.

Minutes Overheard from
The Vagueness Society Holiday Party

NYU Philosophy Department, 1998

Someone is always here to misunderstand us.
This is not the only matter set forth we can save.
No side-step just for moonful eyes, nor blindness
of horses, nor a train's length between sidelong roads.
This is a fugue. We must detail side roads now,
take out the Phrygian mode from our waters.
Truth-values might not be for everybody, but
we can still absolutely hang out here—
hideous, muck-licked against the fake wood walls.
For lo, fellow members, every day is a challenge, we guess.
We were never in the right place or in the right drama.
Someone was always here standing still and said
how we looked like we knew what we were doing.
Blink your eyes and a heap is a non-heap.
Blink your eyes and it's a whole decade and change.
And we would never open their mail.
Their problems are nasty. We dreamt about it, lost it,
forgot it, winced. For we are the most important problem
on Bullshit Row. Anyone next to us looks just like us
with just a little change, and right on down the line until
we are unrecognizable, freaks with our heads cut off.
One must stand up to the villains of certainty and,
in our dotage, we will be paid well to be cranky.
Our sand-heap counsel stays in cages. Blink your eyes
and, generally, vagueness is actually useful. As for the cake:
we didn't eat anything that didn't say it was food before we ate it.

Pompous Symmetry

U2, "Stay (Faraway, So Close!)" (1993)

all the young Jesuses look the same // and that's why I'm afraid // of deserts // because we're obsessed // with trust // we're obsessed // with origin stories // the guns I shot // out in the desert // the saguaros // that ripped flesh // and because I can't stop // getting caught in moshes // all the young Jesuses look the same // and that's why // this extermination // of meaning // sticks to my hands // it's the pompous symmetry // of desert towns // the self-reliance // the fairy tales // sticks to my hands // to put on *Zooropa* or *Achtung Baby* // that is the question // on the drive home // I try to forget // how to build a house // I try to forget // saying I don't need anybody // out in the desert // while tanks of water // tanks of supplies // roll in on trains.

so that's why // I'm afraid // of the desert // and all the young Jesuses // look the same.

Abandoned RCA Buildings, Camden, NJ

The corner of Cooper   and the Delaware River   is stuck in between   my life
and time   The boarded-up buildings   with stained-glass Nippers   echoes
of Caruso   early Sinatra   but this time the darkness   simply looks
back   this time my life is   lost in fruit trees

I've walked each street   in shards of torn denim   I've watched my face
grow old tonight   and I stand on this mound   and   try   to   forget
and continue to flourish   all passers-by   a man gets a match   another
directions   a leashless dog   glimmers and breathes   I preside on this
corner   in sole ministration   stumbling on rocks   in stickerbush patches
I have no hankering   for occupied buildings   and signal to inmates   up
to the prison   and flail with a speech   known only to wives   I rumble and
pass   the steel-latticed fences   and wait for a single   decent idea   and
one came across   as one often does   the night the clock tower   lit up too
early   out of synch with the sun   and for the minute possessed
my life in a shell   the numbers behind   the broken clock tower   death being light   and after the light   time being light   Simple as that   the city
hall tower   was death and time   in tandem together   was death and time
in darkness and light   thinking of Whitman   dead by the river   thinking
of Rutgers   my pot-clouded lectures   the years I spent here   sleeping and
reading   confusion at 20   whole brackets of time   crying and fucking   in
chorus together   daytime malinger   staying inside   and right before that
daylight despair   that's what I said   daylight despair   Please try to follow
just what I'm saying   I found my old corner   utterly silent   one string of
lights   the invincible city   I lived here once   a sad-faced apprentice   I
walked and returned   to silence my words

It's Raining Spiders in Brazil

The Presidents of the United States of America, "Peaches" (1995)

When you're 35, for example, it's about not saying phrases like "the thrum of truth." These things are not merely epistolary. It's about a tradition of stories where someone leaves a body. People don't remember how we played dead among the real dead. Now it's all like un-select the new option so they can't see you. This can't be more prideful than it already is, but it turns out you wouldn't know about it and you still don't know. So. How do we keep baby Jesus in the manger? Armies of characters still cling to completing the voyage in a gregarious and gamely style. If you stare at Trenton long enough, it will go away.

Sometimes it's not an earth-shattering moment.
It's raining spiders in Brazil.

Poem Beginning with 1.5 Lines
from Stupid Idiot Person Joe Rogan

NewsRadio, 1995

Do you know the expression it's better to be a warrior in a garden
than a gardener in a war? Are you familiar with the dictum,
it's cooler to be an axe murderer in the metaverse than a metaverser
with an axe? Do you know the saying, it's more convenient to be a drag queen
at Sephora than a Donnie Darko at Spencer's? Or how about the one
that goes it's way cooler to be a drifter born to walk alone than to be
a loner born with driftwood? Can you dig the ancient saying that it's smarter
to be dilettante who lurks in a food court than a debutant
who deep-throats a corn dog? That, and it's simpler to be a neoliberal on Reddit
than a thinkfluencer on Ron Silliman's blog? Indulge me as I
break out the old chestnut, is it less creepy to be a frat boy in the desert
than a dessert at a frat party? Do you know the truism
it's smarter to be a critic at Book Expo than to be Bruce Kulick on a Kiss Kruise?
Consider the platitude, it's more fulfilling to be a freakazoid on a gentrified
   block
than a gentrifier with a flirtatious streak? Are you acquainted with the
   catchphrase
it's better to be a sweetheart at a swap meet than a meathead at a sweet shop?
Do you know the expression it's more career-friendly to be a nutjob with a
   microphone
or a rubbernecker in a firing squad than a less awful person?

to the heckler at my first poetry reading, 1994

and i can still remember // how you waited // until i finished // each // poem //
to shout // YOU SUCK! // after each // last line // i peeked past // the spotlight
// past the polite // applause from friends // i can still make out // your red hair //
strands over flannel // i can still piece together // a vision // of some // charles //
bukowski // clone // which // in '94 // would mean you were // any male poet //
in philly // you waited // to shout // THAT POEM FUCKIN SUCKED! // and no
one // put an end // to your act // no one // grabbed your arm // and i // gave up
early // i resigned to sharing // the tin angel stage // with your yuengling clinks
// your clean work boots // and i can still hear // your nasal voice // a voice that //
crowd-surfed over the bar // after a poem // about miles davis // the day he died
// you shouted // MILES DAVIS // WOULD'VE HATED // THAT POEM! // and
ok // maybe you were right // mister heckler // i think // decades later // maybe
you // are some evil twin // all i know // years later // is i am not // the narrator //
and i am not the speaker // if i ever was // what i am // is the bitter old man // and
you // you are the bug-eyed // spliff-smoker // the one who went to // the pricey
art college // downtown // and after that night // for weeks // maybe months
// i needed to know // who you were // where you lived // so i could confront
// my redheaded // heckler manchild // but it turns out // you were pals // with
randall "tex" cobb // that's right // the pro boxer // he'd moved to philly // and
you // published his chapbook // of poems // you and tex // would get drunk //
and watch spiderman movies // so even if i // faced you down // even if i // beat
the heckler out of you // you'd sic the retired boxer // the raising arizona guy //
on me // on the way back // from proofreading reports // or drinking beer at
mcglinchey's // he'd roll up // to my spruce street // efficiency // on a motorbike
// smoking a stogie // and pitch grenades // at some bunny // and he'd break my
nose // so // anyway // i'd forgotten you // for years // for decades // i pushed
your face away // until // that is // the other day // when i started this poem //
all i ever // had to do // look you up // and there you are // you and your // por-
cupine red hair // you and your // short guy gut // with photos // of chapbooks
for sale // and darned if you didn't // write a poem // in which // you namedrop

tex // like some // stripmall // frank o'hara // cruising the suburbs // and darned
if your website // doesn't say // you are // available for "lectures, // seminars //
and // readings" // like my grandpop said // christ on a cracker // all i ever // had
to do // was read my email // cos i'll be damned // if you haven't // sent poems
// to little journals // i've edited // over the years // your poems are shitty // for
whatever it's worth // i won't shout it out loud // but i would say here // they are
pickled // in noblesse oblige // but mostly just // the oblige // part // and you
// the shouty // self-promoter // with nothing to say // and more than // 70 //
mutual // friends // on // facebook // and your ratty shirts // arranged just // so
// oh you // the caliban // on my shoulder // art college // dropout // i get that //
my debut // wasn't that great // i mean // in philly // a poet // gets pounced on
// every // day // but //

maybe the worst part // is that //
i remember // you // but you //
you don't remember // me at all

More Poets

after David Trinidad

Just before I had my first book published,
a Poetry Project Poet asked to meet for a drink,
and I thought *great, we're going to be friends.*
I was excited to hang out with a real downtown poet.
He brought a manuscript along to the bar, asked me
to introduce him to my publisher. At the bookstore
reading series I co-ran, a Poet Who Is Now Kind of Famous
took me aside and said, "You're not the first poet
to write about music, you know that, right?"
At the Brooklyn Inn after another bookstore reading,
I handed a Poet Who Begged for a Reading
a check for fifty dollars from Poets & Writers. It took
hours of filling out applications just to get this
little funding. "Well, I guess it's something,"
the Begging Poet grumbled. At a grad program party
in front of several famous poets, a New Grad Student
said, "You remind me of *The Jerry Springer Show.*"
I asked why, and the New Grad Student, who now runs
a major literary organization, said, "Because you look
like you're white trash." Once, after I read
at the Bowery Poetry Club, a Small Press
Publisher went onstage and said he was "so tired
of confessional poems about rock bands" and looked
right at me. So did his wife. After a reading in D.C.,
a Poet Who Is Now a Memoirist walked up to me and said
I had rejected their sestina, but now it was going to be
included in *Best American Poetry*. I said congratulations,

but that didn't seem to be their desired response.
(At every reading for the sestina book I edited, at least
one reader would point out that I had rejected
their sestina for *McSweeney's*.) One morning in SoHo,
excited, I told a Poet Who Would Win a Pulitzer
I had a poem selected for *Best American Poetry*.
Instead of congratulating me or saying something
nice, they stopped and said, as if to themself,
"Jesus, I really need to get my shit together."
And then there was Poet Friend #1, who got mad
when I wrote a short blog post about how a More Famous Poet
stole a story idea I'd pitched to *The Believer*.
It was about poetry and karaoke, and how both
require a certain variety of shamelessness. I didn't
name any names, but just the idea I would complain
and break the chain of famousness enraged Poet Friend #1,
who I'd helped get their book published. Later,
Poet Friend #2 witnessed a Gallery Curator, who
I did not know, throw champagne on me at an opening.
Poet Friends #1 and #2 both figured I deserved it
somehow. After I published an essay on leaving
the New York poetry scene, at AWP in Chicago,
I walked up to say hello to the Editor Who Now Runs
a Major Foundation, but instead of saying hi
they stopped some random strangers, pointed at me,
and said "Hey! This guy wrote about how horrible poets are!"
I once reviewed their partner's book, positively.
I wondered if they knew this had proven my point
in some way. So by the time the Lit Blogger Who Is Now
a Well-Paid Novelist called the leaving New York essay
"terrific (if slightly ingenuous?)" and

"Whether this is a failure of the city, or merely
of the poet, is an open question," I had gotten
so used to things like this being said about my work
that it didn't hurt my feelings. Of course, I'm lying.

Eliot's Religion and a New Way to Screw

Dr. Octagon, *Dr. Octagonecologyst* (1996)

My pitch for a secular church entails just never having to go to church in the first place. That idea died a natural death in Merchantville. And so now I talk about the priest who hated to look at his own face. He really did bring all the sweet fuckery you can imagine, I told him all about my parents' divorce and he thought I was smoking pot because I never washed my contact lenses. And if I ever find god inside some television character, or read that book about how Jesus was a magician, which any tall person can tell just as well, then this story is not as bad as I think it was. It just has to be sung.

Who knows if I'll ever get through all this wisdom literature.
Who the fuck knows.

Debate Outside Four-Faced Liar, 1999

What about sense of play this poet keeps asking me // I guess to pique or troll me about what makes good poetry // *what about sense of play* over and over again in clipped confident chirps // and I am out on the sidewalk bumming smokes on west 4th where a poet-friend tends bar // *what about sense of play* over and over // and I swear I was minding my own business // *what about sense of play* and the poet from new hampshire in a puffed-up pirate shirt won't pipe down // and I pretend not to hear another *what about sense of play* // and I finally say *listen I am just here to see my friends read poems* // but the truth is I couldn't care less about sense of play or fancy or imagination // the truth is I played dumb // and as the subject switched to getting letters of rec for grad school I said

Of course in front of the dildo shop next door. *You're right*, and slipped away into the bar.

The Street Giveth and the Street Taketh Away

Kiss, *Hot in the Shade* (1990)

After twenty years of being complicit and tormented, it was really terrible, and something of a footnote, to unmask an otherwise saintly figure who threw tables at us and punched us in the face. We were driving across the Ben Franklin Bridge. The car skipped two lanes. The Bible wants us to stop telling these stories. The car t-boned ours, a perfect greeting to Philadelphia. What rocks more than black diamonds, anyway? The Bible wants us to stop asking this. Our arms have no part in language. It shifts down to the fist. It's the basic saga, really, the one where we all claim to be victims. As for rocking, or diamonds, well, we became poor when we decided to be writers. Some by choice and some simply resumed the poverty part. So please don't interrupt us while we read your poems. We both know your life could get better. Hint: it won't. Hint: it appears very likely our faith in God interrupts whatever truly tries to speak to us, which is a version of us, of course.

But what we don't want to hear is what's wrong with you.
Let somebody else tell the story. That's what they say.
Because the street giveth and the street taketh away.

From My Desk, c. 1997

And I read poems from old magazines
by people never heard from again.
And I read them all—poems about kites
and maps and turtles, mothers in waiting rooms.
And I mock-gouge my eyes out, head-shakes
above the eggshell pages. And I scold
this grouch in these eye-sockets.
And I open the window to take in
the just-warm breeze. And I wave my head around
as a boy brave-arms from a car, palm-lifts,
boy-hairs ruffled. And I think how air thins out underneath
fast-moving things, and I see my own terrible ideas
vanish in the soft air of Brooklyn. And I think
how this will never get old—more obscure people
will always throw more things up in the air.

Placed into The Abyss

Pavement, "Cut Your Hair" (1994)

Wack jobs workshopped other wack jobs and wondered why a wack job got famous.

For years we added drop shadows to everything—web sites, flyers, metaphors.

They say there's the story and then there's the story about the story.

In the story about the story, I made a habit of smoking beside the East River, even though I didn't smoke.

From notebooks, 1997: "Whatever is taken from space takes up space elsewhere. Reception is not conception."

I have no idea what I meant, of course.

For years I added light copies above darker ones.

In this story about the story, there's always one friend who calls me "darling" just when you need to be called "darling" but you didn't know you needed to be called "darling."

Who would understand that sad young man, anyway?

Prizes, publications, and a career, career, career, career, career, career.

Gary Colemanesque

1. a child star waits to grow into a grotesque version of himself
2. his legs quiver in growth, his eyes pop out, his bright pants tighten, he cries
3. his parents tie him down to a chair and whisper his lines
4. his parents feed him toasted pastries filled with fake fruit
5. a slate claps in front of him, he walks into apple take-charlie take
6. you'd see hoardings of him everywhere outside town
7. a child star grows up to stare at full moons in the daytime and smile
8. his agent sends him commercials, sings him compliments, hangs up
9. his parents loosen the constraints to feed him liquid food
10. a child star waits for his nose to bulge out
11. he will then look like a criminal or a porn star
12. his premature forehead bulges out
13. it is monstrous, and people look away or gawk
14. he stares at the camera when he finishes his lines
15. he takes late flights to Central Virginia to rest up where later he'll marry
16. three people sit down to whisper his lines
17. a child star always memorizes what to say next

On the Meeting of Frank O'Hara
and David Lee Roth

after Philip Levine's "On the Meeting of Garcia Lorca and Hart Crane," 1992

Greenwich Village, 1961. Of course Frank's loaded, and has no clue this seven-year-old will grow up to be the lead singer of Van Halen. Manny Roth welcomes his nephew to Café Wha? He sets him on a stool. A steel drummer sings calypso. David Lee bumps into Frank, who stumbles in from the San Remo after hours of gossiping with abstract expressionists.

No one is of their right mind. Folk singers haggle with Manny over stage time. David joins the hootenanny, sings along. His uncle tells him *don't be humble, kid—you're not that good.*

No poem will come from this chance meeting on MacDougal Street, if it ever did. But have you ever discovered that two giants walked the same exact block, on the same day in New York City, and wondered if the world changed? That, if something like that can happen, God really does exist? That, if something like that can happen, it explains why myths always win in the end?

To review: in 1961, the future lead singer of Van Halen and son of a doctor in Beverly Hills visits his uncle Manny Roth and has his first taste of the stage. Also in 1961, three years before he dies, a poet drinks in that same neighborhood. Did they really meet? Did Frank ever step inside a folk bar, maybe to attend to his boredom? Frank will still collapse on Fire Island. The future Diamond Dave will kick his legs up and sing about ice cream men. He will act like he has forgotten the words to his own songs, and how the only people who put iced tea in their whiskey bottles is The Clash.

I don't want to make this any more than it is. But I can't help myself. I also don't want to cover this story with more earth and grass and prose, and hide what this is really about, which is how I wished for the meeting of these two humans, both too wild for their imaginations, and yet cannot shake this idea of how I might die without having written at least one perfect poem about a city that defeated me over the course of twelve years, and yet could withstand this pair of lunatics without even capturing one biographer's imagination, even as a footnote.

All I've ever done is sing along.

Gethsemane

Jerry Maguire (1998, Cameron Crowe, dir.)

"I'm taller than Jesus," my daughter announces.
I guess she announces this to me, since I am standing
there, next to her, and we're both inside this sculpture park
dotted with abstract figures, and I want to ask her how
she knows, but I haven't had enough coffee
to go spelunking inside the teenage mind. We named
our first born Miriam because we thought
it meant "wished for child," and it does,
and she is, but these days other meanings—
"strong waters" and "rebellion"—apply more.
The wind smacks on gaudy boulders
that look like giant Skittles. I should have asked her
why she even cares that she's taller than the messiah—
I mean, she's an atheist, or irreligious, or whatever
she wants to call herself, and anyway
it feels as if I am working out the differences
between exegesis and hermeneutics, or
apportions and mergers, or facts and this field
we're walking in, an art park founded by
the co-op king of New York. So as we pass
an installation of cartoon clouds held up
by a matrix of beams, I can't help but change
the subject in my mind, and speculate to myself that
this 120 acres of art-filled earth is probably
one big tax write-off, and those metal

effigies of sky might crash down on

our heathen torsos if I mention Jesus again.

"I bet you're probably taller than Tom Cruise,"

I say at last. "What's a Tom Cruise?" she asks.

Late August

Jeff Buckley, *Grace* (1994)

I'm waiting for my father to die. I'm reduced to events strung together. How do you become a prophet? Summer's over. I'm off to school. I'm reduced to this sum of events and that feels fine. The days get shorter, summer's over. I'm off to school, where they got my classrooms all wrong. That's fine. I feel the days growing short. Does that mean I'm a prophet?

Summer's done.
I'm off, helplessly, to school.
I'm waiting for my father to die.

On Realizing Poison's "Every Rose Has Its Thorn" Has the Same Chords as the Replacements' "Here Comes a Regular"

Of course we're always disappointed
on some level, and since of course we know
the opposite of logic is regret,
by which we mean the act of regretting,
and therefore the prototype of heartache
are songs about cowboys who sing sad songs,
which is to say that for each brainy kid
who flips through Edith Hamilton
there is a freak who looks for certain
kinds of danger, but not the usual stuff,
to wit, epic snafus or wrecked careers,
we're talking about the opposite of bluffing,
which is betrayal, by which we mean the act
of betraying, and a sad cowboy song
will always break you down, irregardless
of one's cowboy status, just like
the opposite of myth is description,
which is to say the act of describing,
or why every Greek maiden pulls a double-cross,
or every poor god gets tied down to a rock
or turned into a cow, to which I would add
every barfly I've ever met will croon
along to Don McLean to drown out
a rehash of their fuck-ups, which is to say,
short story long, that every barfly to whom
I've told a joke says they've heard the joke
before, which is to say the opposite of a poem is
just like the ache for one more poem like it.

ACKNOWLEDGMENTS

Thank you to the editors of the following publications for giving these poems their first home, often in different form:

3am Magazine: "Hot Blooded"

American Poetry Review: "Poem Written at Pete's Candy Store Ending with Line from 'Ray of Light'"; "Nostalgia Ain't What It Used to Be"; "Pompous Symmetry"

Bennington Review: "The Failed Saratoga Colonic Fable"

The Collagist: "Two 90s Poetry Readings"

Court Green: "[I can't even say punk was important, even as it happened,]"; "On the Meeting of Frank O'Hara and David Lee Roth"; "Hello, Dolly"; "Debate Outside Four-Faced Liar"; "This Is Not a List Poem"

The Daily Drunk: "Placed into The Abyss: After Pavement's 'Cut Your Hair'"; "Lines composed after being told by a poet I should 'go out in nature more often and look at chipmunks'"; "A List of Famous People I Saw in New York City, c. 1994-2001"

Diode Poetry Journal: "Poem Beginning with 1.5 Lines from Stupid Idiot Person Joe Rogan"

Electric Literature's The Commuter: "The death of college rock: September 5, 1995"; "On Realizing Poison's 'Every Rose Has Its Thorn' Has the Same Chords as the Replacements' 'Here Comes a Regular'"

Failbetter: "Gary Colemanesque"

FreezeRay Poetry: "Wallace Stevens' Lost *Road House* Commentary"

Good Men Project: "Gethsemane"

Gulf Coast: "From My Desk"

The Harpoon Review: "The Street Giveth and the Street Taketh Away"

The Hopkins Review: "Looks That Kill"

Matter: "Minutes Overheard from The Vagueness"

Society Holiday Party"; "Future Days"

Mr. Beller's Neighborhood: "October 3, 1995"

Mutiny!: "Fable Written While Listening to Alternative Country Rock and Just
    Not Feeling It"; "It's Raining Spiders in Brazil"; "Eliot's Religion and a New
    Way to Screw"

New York Press: "Mott Street Pastoral"

Red Fez: "1998: The Drummer in Our Band Tells Us He's a Virgin"; "The Last
    Days of Childhood"

Right Hand Pointing: "Eavesfall"

Tribes: "Künstlerroman, 1996"; "Lower Broadway Wednesdays, 1997-1999"

Unbroken: "The Art of Prose (With Digressions)"

Unlost: "Nineties Catchphrase Cento Sonnet"

What Rough Beast: "The Plan Shifted with a Ferocious Snap"; "To the Protest
    Song Industry in Crisis"

Word For/Word: "I Tell These Stories To Explain Why People Stop Liking Me";
    "That Twat with Jazz Hands Won't Stop Dancing"

XConnect: "Abandoned RCA Buildings, Camden, NJ"

"Late August" was part of David Kirschenbaum's "August Project" collaboration.

This book was a long time coming. Thank you first and foremost to Michael
Broder for giving this manuscript a home and a space in the world, and for taking
me out of poetry retirement many years ago. Thank you to Matthew Lippman,
Tracey Knapp, and Virginia Konchan for being awesome poets, for writing nice
things about this book, but mostly for being great people in general. Thank you
and love to Maisie Weissman, love of my life, my wife and partner, for supporting
me in every way, and to our daughters, Miriam Nester and Beatrice Nester, for
being kinda interested in what I do. Thank you to students and colleagues at
The College of Saint Rose, who have given me space to explore poems and prose
and to try out drafts and ideas over the years. Thank you to the fellow travelers
on the writing circuit-journey, who encourage, take me seriously, and inspire me:
Michael McNally-Costello, Jonathan Silverman, Jen Hyde, Richard Eoin Nash,
Geoffrey Gatza, Patty Paine, Jeffrey Morgan, Dale Wisely, Michael Schiavo, Jan-

et Dale, Todd J. Colby, Afaa Michael Weaver, Aaron Belz, Jill Ivey, Bob Holman, Cristin O'Keefe Aptowicz, Derrick Brown, Rone Shavers, Jonah Winter, Sonya Huber, Dan Long, January O'Neil, Stephen Allen May, Christoph Paul, Patrick W. Gallagher, Shira Dentz, Jennifer Epstein, Rachel Shukert, Stephen Furlong, Shappy Seasholtz, Shafer Hall, Marc Eliot Stein, George Murray, Alexis Bhagat, Jason Schneiderman, Michael Peters, Amy Fusselman, W. Bliem Kern, David Lehman, Alex Tunney, Gregory Pardlo, Shawn Berman, Crystal Durant, Jonathan Minton, Christine Scanlon, Danny Shot, Diane Wakoski, Blaise Allysen Kearsley, Ernie Hilbert, Carley Moore, Marion Wrenn, Thomas Beller, Thomas V. Hartmann, Thom Didato, David Yezzi, Douglas Rothschild, Tony Trigilio, David Trinidad, and Jackie Sheeler (rest in peace).